T0122143

Moonbeam Tracks

Written By:
Carmelle Thorfinnson Cant
Illustrated By:
Patricia Winnett

www.carmellethorfinnsoncant.com
Library of Congress Control Number: 2017914062

ISBN: Softcover 978-1-5434-0395-4
Hardcover 978-1-5434-0396-1
EBook 978-1-5434-0394-7

Print information available on the last page

Rev. date: 09/13/2018

To order additional copies of this book, contact:
Xlibris
1-800-455-039
www.xlibris.com.au
Orders@Xlibris.com.au

I dedicate this book to
the memory of Richard
and to my grandsons
William, Tobey and Samuel

Acknowledgements

I wish to thank for their support and encouragement, family and friends especially my husband Sam and my sister in law Lynda Kaye.

To my daughter Adrienne who acted as my agent and toiled for countless hours to get things just right, I give my heartfelt thanks. It truly was a labour of love.

To friend and artist Patricia Winnett, a big thank you for many enjoyable "working lunches" and for faithfully capturing in pictures, what I sought to convey in words.

Bunyip Billabong

When I went to the billabong
I saw a bunyip print
The footprint of a bunyip
is bigger than you think.

I looked into the bushes
and saw a pair of eyes
I thought it was a bunyip
wearing a disguise

I heard a sort of rustling
in amongst the leaves
It was so very scary
I got shaky at the knees

But then I saw a floppy ear,
a whisker and a tail
and out jumped my friend Tommy
with his big dog Abigail

Emu

An emu with a beady eye
is hungry for a piece of pie
a sandwich or some cake would do
Take care or she'll steal
your lunch from you !

My doggie and me

We go for a walk
my doggie and me
He sniffs at every post and tree
Getting messages I cannot see
Meant for dogs and not for me

Invisible graffiti

Slippery Fish

The slippery fishes of
Port Phillip bay
swim in the waves
all the long day
Under the seaweed,
down deep where it's cool
the slippery fishes swim in a school

Learning

At Ayers Rock I learned to walk

In Shepparton I learned to run

In Esperance I leaned to dance

In Whitsunday I learned to play

In Gundegai I learned to fly

In Bendigo I learned to sew

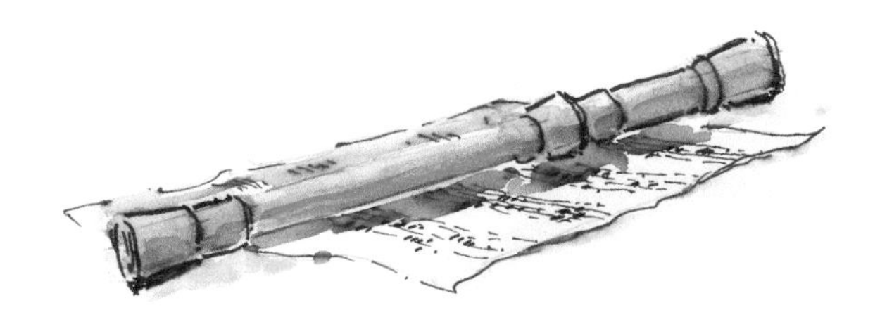

In Wollongong
I learned a song

And I learned to swim and I learned to dive
in Noosa and Coolangatta

Bush Creatures

A wombat is big and fat
a tiger snake is lean
a parakeet is very sweet
a crocodile is mean

An emu bird can't even fly
but a sugar glider can
a lyre bird is very shy
and hides behind his fan

A kangaroo can jump quite far
then stops to take a rest
Of all the creatures in the bush
I like the koala best

Hands

Think of the things our hands can do
They can button a coat and tie up a shoe

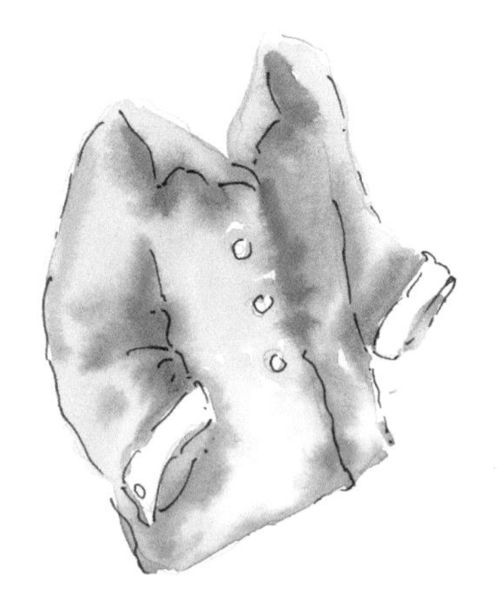

They can catch a ball and
throw a stick

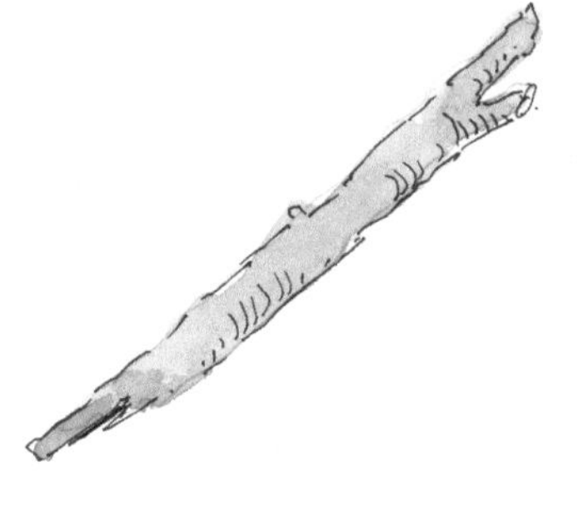

and even do a magic trick

They can push a button or scratch our head

spoon up yoghurt and butter bread

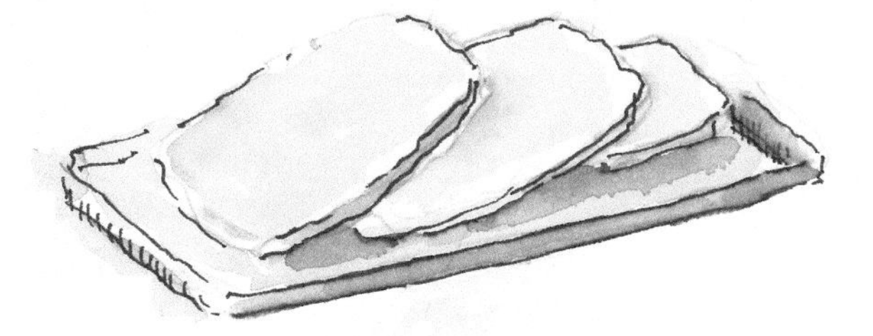

Turn a knob and wave goodbye

And wipe away a tear from our eye

My little dog

My little dog is very charming
although his bark may be alarming
He warns me of all sorts of dangers
Like sudden noise and passing strangers

Then he has other chores to do
Like chasing a ball or chewing a shoe
He jumps to sit in the window wide
and barks at the birds on the lawn outside

He goes to dig in the garden bed
Back inside – time to be fed
Then curls up for a cosy sleep
a little heartbeat at my feet.

Clothes of Sunlight

I dressed myself in sunlight
it lasted for a day

I dressed myself in moonlight
it faded fast away

I dressed myself in windy gales
they blew off in a storm

I dressed myself in happy thoughts
those clothes have kept me warm

Busy Bee

I looked into a flower
and saw a busy bee
He was so very busy
he didn't notice me

He had yellow pollen boots
and stripes upon his back
and when I looked more closely
I saw a little stack

Of tiny bee – school booklets
all tied up in a pack.
He held it very tightly underneath his wing
and when I listened carefully
I thought I heard him sing

"I go to bee school every day
to learn a thing or two
Like how to keep my feet dry
in the early morning dew"

"And how to gather honey from
a snap dragon that snaps
and how to get home safely when
I hear the thunder claps"

Funny Feet

From under the gate I can see the street
and look at all the passing feet
Some shoes are big and some are small
Some feet aren't wearing shoes at all

Gum boots and sandals, sports shoes and slippers
I even saw some bright blue flippers

Those big black boots belong to a man
are the little white shoes going to see "Gran"?

They're all in a hurry to get somewhere
But what will they do when they get there?
Will they jump and run as fast as they're able
Or sit down to tea tucked under a table?

Firefly

Firefly with your blinking light
Blink your way to my house tonight
Bring your friends and make a glow
A kind of magical fireworks show

Alien

An alien from outer space
came to earth to run a race
He said "If I run on a moonbeam track
I could probably get to the moon and back,
or even as far as planet Mars
if I dodge around two or three stars"

Then up he jumped and off he flew;
where he went, nobody knew
But sometimes at night when I look at the stars
I think I can see him waving from Mars

I like

I like the feel of raindrops on my nose
and sand between my toes

I like the smell of biscuits when they're baking
and popcorn in the making

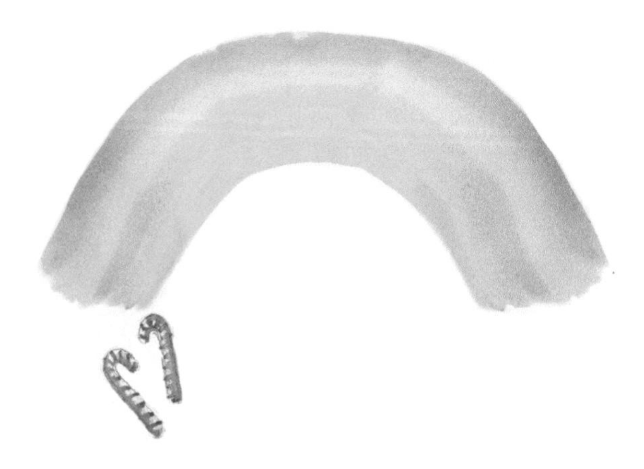

I like the look of stripy candy canes
and rainbows when it rains

I like the taste of vegemite on bread
or a cheesy roll instead

I like the sound of doorbells
when they're ringing
and magpies when they're singing

I like to think of family and fun
and picnics in the sun

I like to think of my warm and cosy bed
and a pillow for my head

It's getting late .... turn off the light
It's time for me to say goodnight.

GOOD NIGHT !

Blue Dark

The day turns into blue-dark night
before the moon comes out

The shadows all have gone to bed
there are no birds about

The silent clouds drift slowly by
the stars begin to peep

The earth is getting ready for its
hours of rest and sleep

Printed in the United States
By Bookmasters